# Where Are Prairie Dogs?

Mary Beth Crum and Fay Robinson
Illustrated by John Palacios

# Contents

Rigby®

# Chapter 1
## Summer with Grandpa

Maria and her brother Javier would spend every summer with their grandpa. He lived in a cozy, two-story home in Colorado. They looked excitedly out the window as their plane got ready to land.

"I can't wait to see Grandpa again!" said Javier.

"I can't wait to see Grandpa *and* the prairie dogs again!" exclaimed Maria.

Maria and Javier got off the plane and rushed into Grandpa's open arms. "It's so good to see you again!" said Grandpa, hugging them both.

Grandpa's shirt smelled like fresh air, as if he spent all of his time outdoors. His hug made Maria feel warm and safe.

"I can't wait to see the prairie dogs!" she said.

"Well, some things have changed around here," Grandpa said sadly, "but we should still be able to see a few prairie dogs."

"How have things changed?" asked Javier.

"You'll understand when we get out to the prairie," said Grandpa.

The car ride was hot and dusty, but Maria and Javier didn't care because they were thrilled to be with their grandpa. Soon they left the city, and patches of green grass and flowers began to appear outside.

But there were also new houses and crowded streets with shopping malls covering what used to be big parts of the wide, open prairie.

"Isn't this where we used to watch the prairie dogs play?" asked Javier.

"Yes, it is, but the prairie is much smaller now," Grandpa explained.

"I think I see a prairie dog!" called Maria, pointing out the car window.

# Chapter 2
# Prairie Dogs' Worst Enemy

Grandpa stopped the car, and they all got out. Quietly they crept closer to a mound of dirt near the road where they saw a prairie dog standing very still on its back legs.

"I think that it's guarding its family inside the hole," whispered Javier.

"Look," said Maria, pointing, "I see some more prairie dogs over there."

Suddenly a bulldozer started its engine with a loud roar. A prairie dog barked a couple of loud yipping barks, and soon other prairie dogs joined in. Then, all at once, they dove head first into their holes.

"The barking prairie dogs are letting all of the other prairie dogs know that danger is nearby," said Grandpa.

Maria searched the rolling hills for hawks and foxes. (She knew that hawks and foxes liked to eat prairie dogs.) When she didn't see any, she asked Grandpa what the prairie dogs were afraid of.

"Hawks and foxes aren't the only danger to prairie dogs," explained Grandpa. "Did you know that humans have become the prairie dogs' worst threat? People are building things on the prairie dogs' land and destroying their homes. And it's not just the prairie dogs that are being harmed. Black-footed ferrets and other prairie animals are in danger, too!"

Maria knew they had to do something to save the prairie dogs from becoming homeless, so she asked Grandpa for his help.

# Chapter 3
# Time to Make a Plan

"I'll go and talk to the man on the bulldozer," said Grandpa. "Maybe he can stop working for a while until we can come up with a plan for these little animals."

When Grandpa walked away, Javier and Maria giggled as they watched the prairie dogs peek their furry heads out of their holes.

"I think that they're checking to see if it's safe to come out," said Maria. One by one, the little prairie dogs came out of their holes.

"Javier, do you think prairie dogs will become extinct like the dinosaurs?" asked Maria, who was becoming more and more concerned.

"I hope not, because that would be terrible!" cried Javier.

Grandpa looked upset as he walked back from the bulldozer. "Well, the man said that he is done for now but the bulldozer and the builders will return in two weeks to begin building a store here."

"Then we need to create a plan, and we need to do it fast!" exclaimed Maria.

Grandpa told Maria and Javier about his friend who worked with a group that rescued prairie dogs. Grandpa promised to call his friend, Mr. Thomas, after dinner that night.

That night Maria waited nervously while
Grandpa talked to Mr. Thomas on the phone.

"What did he say?" Maria asked hopefully
when Grandpa finally hung up.

Grandpa looked concerned as he considered
the amount of work needed to save the prairie
dogs. He hoped the kids were ready!

# Chapter 4
# Ready to Help

Grandpa told Maria and Javier about his phone call.

"Mr. Thomas said that he will visit the prairie Monday morning and figure out how many prairie dogs live there. Then he will need to get traps, a truck, and a group of people to help. He also needs to find a new home for the prairie dogs!"

"That's so much to do! Will he be able to do it all in two weeks?" asked Maria.

"I really hope so," said Grandpa as he smiled at Maria.

To make the time go more quickly while they waited to hear from Mr. Thomas, Maria and Javier learned as much as they could about moving the prairie dogs. They looked up information on the Internet and borrowed books from the library.

Finally Grandpa got a call from Mr. Thomas. "Mr. Thomas was able to gather the people and supplies needed to move the prairie dogs!" reported Grandpa. "We can join him Monday morning to help him and his group move them."

Maria and Javier both shouted, "Yes!" at the same time.

Maria, Javier, and Grandpa arrived at the prairie just as Mr. Thomas drove up in a big truck. Other people came and began taking the prairie dog traps off the truck and placing them near the holes. Mr. Thomas explained that the traps did not hurt the prairie dogs but were good places to keep the prairie dogs safe for a short time.

"Thank you so much for doing this quickly," Grandpa said to Mr. Thomas.

"I'm happy to do it," said Mr. Thomas. "The prairie dogs are helpless animals, and they don't have the ability to fight back when people take over the prairies and destroy their homes. The food and shelter they need is here on the prairie."

# Chapter 5
# Waiting for a Prairie Dog

Maria walked over to Mr. Thomas, ready to help. "What can I do to help the prairie dogs, Mr. Thomas?" offered Maria.

"Maria, you can put the bait in this trap," he answered.

Mr. Thomas showed her the buckets of horse food, which they used to bring the prairie dogs out of their holes.

Carefully Maria put a handful of horse food inside a metal trap that looked like a little cage.

"Watch the trap and let me know as soon as you see a prairie dog dart into it," instructed Mr. Thomas.

The group waited for more than an hour, but no prairie dogs appeared.

"What if they're too fearful to come out?" Maria whispered to Javier.

Javier thought for a second and then answered, "We'll just keep waiting until they feel safe enough to come out."

Finally one of the prairie dogs crawled out of its hole, looked around, and noticed the food in the trap. Maria held her breath so that she wouldn't make a sound and scare the prairie dog back into its hole.

The prairie dog slipped inside the trap to nibble the food, and SNAP! The door came down.

"Mr. Thomas, there's a prairie dog inside my cage!" called Maria.

"Be very careful so that you don't upset it," warned Mr. Thomas.

He pulled out a cloth and covered most of the cage with it, explaining that the cloth would protect the prairie dog from the sun and help it stay calm. Then he picked up the cage and carried it to his truck.

By that afternoon, the truck was filled with five covered cages. Happy with their success, the helpers got into their cars and followed the truck to the prairie dogs' new home in a different, open area of prairie.

Maria watched as the adults placed the cages on the ground. They opened one cage at a time and waited for the prairie dogs to run onto their new land.

# Chapter 6
# A Job Well Done

"I'm so tired, but I know our effort was worth it!" said Maria as she watched all the prairie dogs play and run around the hills of their new prairie.

"Absolutely," agreed Javier.

"We did some wonderful work today," said Grandpa.

Maria and Javier knew they would have a good night's sleep.

At dinner that night, Maria could hardly stay awake.

"Mr. Thomas gave me these forms," said Javier. "We need to ask people here in Colorado to sign them and send them to the lawmakers. Maybe then they will change some of the laws about building on prairies. That would help save some more prairie dogs."

"I can't wait to get back to school in a couple of months to tell everyone what we did for the prairie dogs this summer," Maria said, yawning.

"Maybe the people where you live can help, too," said Grandpa.

"Some humans may be prairie dogs' worst
enemies, but *this* human is their best friend!"
said Maria, pointing to herself.

"You certainly are," said Grandpa, giving her
a big hug.

Grandpa carried her to her bed and
whispered, "Good night," but Maria was already
dreaming about happy little prairie dogs
scurrying in and out of the holes of their
new home.